The Lone Sailboat
Navigating in Political Waters

Edward Korczynski

Outskirts Press, Inc.
http://www.outskirtspress.com

ISBN: 978-1-9772-4347-8

Cover Image: Storm on the Sea of Galilee, Rembrandt, 1633.
Title Page Image: The Lone Sailboat, Anne Lombardo, 2020.
All rights reserved - used with permission.

Outskirts Press and the "OP" logo are trademarks belonging to Outskirts Press, Inc.

PRINTED IN THE UNITED STATES OF AMERICA

Preface: Navigating in Political Waters | i

Life and Society | 1

Culture	1	
Values	4	
Conscience	9	
Defense of Life	10	
Abortion	12	
Marriage	15	
Gender	17	

That Which Matters | 21

Family	21	
Friendship	25	
Failure & Success	25	

Government | 29

The U.S. Constitution and the Establishment Clause	30	
Military Service	33	
Immigration	34	
Capitalism	37	
Health Care	38	

Church/Religion | 47

Mercy and Forgiveness	52	
Sin	53	
Time	55	
Prayer	55	
Death	56	
The Bible	57	
God	58	

The Arts & Sciences | 61

Mathematics	61	
Science	62	
Literature	62	
Art	62	
Music	63	

Education | 65

A Brief Word | 71

PREFACE:
NAVIGATING IN POLITICAL WATERS

From what were once wet-lands, slowly but inexorably a marina emerged. It took millennia, but now it is a tranquil retreat; luckily, it is adjacent to an equally quiet and sleepy little town on the south side of a river which flows into the bay. It is from this idyllic spot that we backed out of our slip, slowly motored out of the marina onto the river and headed for the bay. Headed into the wind, we unfurled the main and the jib, fell off, cut the engine and headed south.

In the Northeast, Memorial Day is considered the unofficial beginning of summer while Labor Day signals summer's end. On a Thursday after Labor Day we found ourselves sailing south down the bay. We were alone—not a boat in sight. School had started, the vacationers were gone, and the locals, well, they were at their favorite spots which were finally free from noise and crowds.

Sailing provides quiet. A casual observer might imagine that sailing is a boring and terribly lugubrious activity, taking an interminable amount of time to reach any destination. But sailors are not interested in speed (unless racing!). They are interested in the journey, precisely because it provides time for reflection and contemplation. The image of the skipper at the helm, idle and at the mercy of the prevailing wind is deceptive. It takes some work at times, but by tacking, a skilled sailor can reach his destination, even in an unfavorable wind.

An initial observation of sailors, whether solo or in the company of others, is a keen awareness of being alone on a force of nature. Sometimes they sail alone on a sea which can either be a perfect gentleman or a raging beast. Lightning, wind, rain, rogue waves, equipment failure or sickness can cause severe problems. On occasion a hurricane or rough weather can precipitate disaster at a normally serene home port. The physical challenges presented by the naturally occurring conditions must be addressed as they occur. Knowledge and the ability to remain calm are crucial elements of success.

The feeling of being alone at sea, and the challenges it presents, is a mirror image of what we face in our daily lives. In life the challenges are psychological and moral as well as physical. They must be faced and addressed on a constant basis or we become overwhelmed. While a storm may rage at sea, it eventually passes and calm is restored. The battle we are in daily is constant—both in the public square and at home. The enemy we face is evil. This most formidable adversary is relentless, insidious, brilliant, unapologetic and tireless in its effort to destroy. It is at our peril that we fail to call out and combat evil in its minutia. For evil attacks in imperceptible increments, hoping we will ignore little insignificant adjustments until we are overwhelmed and defeated. Vigilance is necessary. Responding in the public square is critical but responding with knowledge and courage has been lacking. We can easily see this failure's deleterious effects on our culture as it has led to a decline in the quality of our society. Maintenance of a moral society is even more important than the maintenance of societal infrastructure.

The source of all moral beliefs is God; that is to say what we believe is true precisely because it emanates from God. Thus, our beliefs are founded in truth, rather than in common human knowledge or wisdom. When we advocate for something we rely on God's truth rather than human opinion or feeling. When practical morality based on truth declines in a society, all else in the societal structure will follow suit.

In life we do not face physical storms on a daily basis but rather storms which are much more dangerous. Storms which, if not confronted directly and immediately, will destroy our character, dignity, morality and humanity. So, out of my private world I step into the public square to address issues which, in my view, have been inadequately addressed by the authorities:

- Those I have counted on to be the watchdogs;
- Those I have counted on to promote truth and beauty;
- Those I have counted on to promote the general welfare;
- Those I have counted on to advance the will of God on earth;
- Those I have counted on and repeatedly found lacking.

I will mention the issue of abortion several times in these pages; I do not want to leave you with the impression that I am interested in only one issue. Abortion is so critical for many reasons, and all of them have to do with what we are doing to ourselves: Abortion is about death. Put more bluntly, it is about the murder of children. The numbers are staggering. Worldwide, there are approximately 44,000 abortions per day—over 16,000,000 abortions per year. In the United States the approximate numbers are 1,788 abortions per day—over 650,000 per year. This procedure is being performed on innocent, defenseless and voiceless babies. They can't object— they are completely vulnerable and therefore easy targets. The God of the Universe will hold all of us responsible for this, including me.

If you are in favor of abortion, consider the following: Imagine the world without you in it; all of your joys prompted by physical and intellectual accomplishments; the love you have for your parents, wife, children, and friends; the joys of reading, art, literature, music and athletics never occurred because one or both of your parents decided to abort you for convenience sake. This is the sentence you pronounce for the unborn when you abort. Among Catholic politicians who favor abortion, the sophisticated argument has been couched this way: "While I am personally opposed to abortion, I do not want to force my opinion on others." The logic of this argument is absolutely bankrupt. Their next sentence should be: "While I personally support a particular issue, I do not want to force my opinion on others." The result would be that these politicians would do nothing. Perhaps that is what pertains. The other absurd logical argument it presents can be categorized this way: "I am personally opposed to murder, rape, slavery, oppression and prejudice, but I do not want to force my opinions on others." If this is the logic by which Catholic politicians who support abortion are operating, they are incompetent and should be removed from office. Catholic Bishops should alert them that they are in danger of excommunication: "What good is it to gain the whole world, and lose one's soul?"

Trigger warning: I will be politically incorrect. At this juncture in life, I couldn't care less about being politically correct.

• • •

As we enter the serpentine channel which takes us out of the inlet, past the lighthouse and out to sea, we lower the sails and motor through for an hour before reaching the open ocean. Here the journey begins – across the sea and beyond.

LIFE AND SOCIETY

Culture

I refer now to culture in the United States of America. We are a mixture of many operating cultural aspects. Some of them are coarse and some lofty. But overall we have a fascinating, vibrant first rate culture. You may disagree, but let me tell you why I think our culture is the best in the world. At times I am extremely disappointed in our culture, especially the popular culture. But, overall I feel ours is the best culture there is because the American people have managed to balance the ideal with the practical in a formula that has worked well—to this point.

We Americans have come from every place on earth. We have arrived here proud of the places from which we have come, but eager to become Americans. We have managed to preserve the best aspects of the cultures we left behind while jettisoning, to a large extent, those aspects which were onerous. This cultural churn has played a large part in the success of the United States, especially in creating our highly successful culture. Culture is fragile; it must be carefully guarded. It can slip away as easily as water cupped in ones hands, if the fingers are inadvertently separated. And it can slip away, unnoticed, one minute drop at a time, until it reaches an arid land of no return.

The bases of our culture are the Declaration of Independence and the Constitution. The knowledge and wisdom of the men who wrote those documents originated from long standing religious principles. And those principles are still at work in this country. Various religious traditions function independently and in cooperation with one another, providing a vital thread in the fabric of the nation. We are still a very young culture compared to the world's most ancient civilizations, but if we adhere to the principals of both country and faith, our culture will continue to grow, improve and prosper. There are indicators which point to the fact that we have been getting it right. We avoided a blood bath after both the Revolutionary and Civil Wars, which is quite an accomplishment. The blight of slavery was expunged and an honest effort on the part of most Americans to eliminate prejudice continues. All things are subject to improvement; we should remember to be more eager to improve than to condemn.

From where I sit, I see many signs of cultural erosion.

Our body politic does not reflect the mood or thinking of most of the general public. And that is unusual since the political sector is usually a microcosm of what is generally true in the broad society. Currently, there is a significant chasm between the two. Many elected officials, federal, state and local are corrupt, and too many, including judges, abuse the power of their offices. Many violate the Constitution with impunity. Expediency in achieving victory, power and wealth rules the day. The general public is well aware of this, and at present is providing the counter weight. The leadership, in both the Democrat and Republican parties, contrary to what they preach, continues to deficit spend, manipulate the system as far as they can and generally does not reflect the ethos of the country at large. The parties seek only to destroy each other; they find it nearly impossible to acknowledge and support the other party when it has accomplished something that benefits the country. This does not go unnoticed. Individual Americans and the private sector proceed more amicably and the country, despite the behavior of the politicians, is stronger for it. The foolish pronouncements of many top politicians may not always be adequately addressed. But those pronouncements and those who pronounce them are certainly being ignored. The culture continues to grow and the country to prosper on the strength of its people.

Large segments of the press are dishonest, filtering news to promote their own agenda rather than honestly reporting all the facts. Good news is avoided especially if it does not fit the approved narrative. Bad news floods the airwaves, creating the impression that it is the norm. This poor impression, emanating from the press and broadcast media, is misleading. Millions of Americans go to work daily, dedicated to their jobs, families, country, faith, fellow citizens and to the poor and needy throughout the country and the world. Thousands of acts of kindness and charity go unnoticed each day. More money is donated to charity in the United States than in any other country in the world. But the broadcast news is not interested in any of this. It is much easier for them to distribute mediocrity, or even rubbish, than to promote and provide high standard productions. They are in the process of extinguishing the attention of large segments of the general public. News organizations, newspapers, the broadcast media and experts, once respected, are now beginning to be viewed askance. In many cases they are ignored, and are becoming irrelevant. The reason for this is not complex, although it may appear so on the surface. It is the detachment from truth which is eroding the credibility of our public institutions. It is easier to criticize based on hearsay and assumption rather than digging for the facts. And even when the facts are known, in too many cases, emotional and personal biases have the upper hand and truth is abandoned.

Institutions of higher learning, once dedicated to producing well rounded, educated and competent graduates, have allowed themselves to be degraded and diminished by relaxing standards.

Cable companies provide hundreds of channels, most of which are unwatchable. While cable company executives are relaxing with their profits, the nonsense of the programming is being noticed and countered by more and more viewers who are abandoning cable and satellite providers.

Church attendance is down, at least in part, because standards have been relaxed and the teaching watered down. At first this relaxation may please the faithful, but they soon realize they are being fed mush, turn it off and leave.

Values

There is much discussion about values in contemporary America. The definition of "values" is critical to understanding what is meant when the term is used in public discourse. In our popular culture, even among the well-educated, values are changeable—as is "truth." Among those who subscribe to the notion that there is your truth, my truth and many alternate truths, there is no room for an objective standard. But it is precisely an objective standard that determines values. The ultimate objective standard is God. The closer we follow that standard, the closer our values approach truth. And the closer they are to the truth, the less they are subject to whim, fancy or trend. From this point of view, values are behaviors and paths we pursue because they are themselves good and because they produce good results. The definitions of good and good results are in the exclusive domain of the creator; the closer our definitions match His own, the closer we come to the true understanding of what a worthwhile value is. Being able to do so requires attention to scripture, tradition and the magisterium of the Church.

Two paradigms operate concomitantly—one physical and material, the other spiritual. We are subject to the laws of both. The physical/material paradigm is, however, subject to the spiritual paradigm. Mankind can violate both spiritual and physical laws due to the gift of free will. When I refer to values and standards I refer to those which originate in the spiritual paradigm. Spiritual values and standards do not change—they operate whether we acknowledge them or not. They are completely independent and operate only on the volition of God. The standards, for example, of weights and measures are not moral standards; they operate in the physical order. Ultimately, all things are grounded in the spiritual. This is true even of those things which seem only remotely related — or not related at all — to the spiritual. The spiritual laws can be violated when theory is put into practice, but such violations have no effect on objective reality. It will be difficult to reach this conclusion, or even understand it, without having some sort of religious faith.

Time is an important factor in this paradigm: what we find either acceptable or unacceptable today may have been just the opposite a decade ago — or a century or more ago. We often hear that we should not judge the past by the standards of today. This, of course, presupposes that values, truth and standards are mutable and that they change on our whim at any particular point in time. It is a philosophical view with problems. Owning slaves has been a common practice in many cultures. It is not so now. Are we then comfortable with the notion that this could change at some future date? That slave-holding might once again become acceptable? Are we confident that what we consider an improvement now will not change in the future? What prevents a change of any kind if values, truth and standards are malleable? And what are the means by which we judge whether something has improved or declined if we do not admit of an objective reality outside of ourselves which is not influenced by what we think or feel? Is human sacrifice a value simply because it was practiced in the past? Should we refrain from labeling the practice barbaric because our sense of right and wrong has changed? Should we adopt the view that our values are no better or worse than those of the ancients, only different? These questions are easily answered by those who believe in God. Truth does not change when individuals act in a completely subjective atmosphere. But conditions will change. An insight into the fact that values and standards are based on truth, and that the source of truth is God, and therefore immutable, is an ever increasingly dismissed idea. What is morally good has always been so and what is morally objectionable has always been so. Behavior and beliefs change but values, truth and standards, which are based on the law of God, do not. Men are not the ultimate judges; it is God who judges. A large portion of the modern world dismisses this truth.

For example: If we alter a standard, unless the change enhances agreement with truth, the change is detrimental. Changes may occur for many reasons—political opportunity, expediency, convenience, exploitative motives, incompetence—but unless done for the explicit purpose of improvement, they damage those subject to them. An example from education is illustrative.

The point of studying mathematics is to understand the logic of how numbers work and to become proficient in using them. High standards should be set to encourage and produce competency. Some students will not be capable of meeting the standards. To reduce the standards for the purpose of allowing those students to pass with high grades, gives them a false sense of security at best. There is no shame in failing if one is incapable, but there should be great shame on behalf of a system which distorts reality by ostensibly championing an untruth. The notion that all students are equally capable is false. If it were true, we would all be as capable as Einstein, Beethoven or Da Vinci. But we are not all equally capable in that sense. It is a misapplication of providing aid for those in need that induces institutions to lower standards. This attempt to help is well intentioned, but has severe unintended consequences. Lowering standards shifts a smaller, manageable present problem and projects it forward; the further it moves ahead in time the less manageable it becomes. The burden it places on the society will eventually overwhelm it. The practical consequences of lowering standards include:

- A widening gap between rich and poor;
- A higher rate of incompetence among professionals in all fields;
- The decline of technology and innovation;

- Falling away from belief in God; and
- In general, a disgruntled and pessimistic population which perceives its ability to advance as extremely limited.

These are by no means the only negative results of applying such a flawed approach to solving problems. The unintended negative consequences, many of which we are completely unaware, can slowly infiltrate and ruin a society and a nation if not checked.

If we were all equally brilliant, would it lead to more cooperation or more strife? Perhaps the latter, since our nature would remain the same; and that is the source of the problem. Alone, we are incapable of changing our nature. We are all subject to adopting the nonchalant attitude that there has always been corruption, it exists now, and will continue to exist in the future. While this is true, we cannot allow ourselves and our culture to passively accept it. History demonstrates that the eroding of values leads to the decline of civilizations.

There is of course controversy about what is considered a value. For example, there are those who believe Communism is a valuable political system and those who are of the opposite opinion. Are there criteria which can be used to prove which is correct? Since we will be unable to convince a secularist of correctness based on the law of God, we may have to use a different method. Perhaps an empirical method of determining who is correct is possible by utilizing Kant's Categorical Imperative. I do not want to explore all the implications of Kant's philosophy; applying the Imperative in a thought experiment should suffice.

Simply stated, we can take any behavior, make it universal, and then observe the results. If the results are good, we can deem the behavior good; if the results are destructive, we can deem the behavior imprudent and something to be avoided. Let us apply this concept to a prosaic example which will be clear, precise and free—almost universally—from controversy.

If all drivers were to adopt the practice of driving while drunk, the results would be disastrous. That this principle is so universally accepted is evidenced by the fact that laws prohibiting this behavior are in place around the globe. While not all examples are as clearly evident as is this one, it unambiguously demonstrates the point: Since we know the results of such behavior is unacceptable, our effort is to eliminate it completely.

For some, a moral and spiritual reason may not prove sufficiently powerful to influence behavior. In that case, Kant's powerful intellect provides another path: If the moral and spiritual are not sufficient to influence behavior, perhaps a logical and empirical argument will do the trick. While the former will seem remote and unfamiliar to many, the latter are concrete and familiar to almost all.

More of mankind would probably be persuaded not to jump off the Empire State Building because of awareness of the physical consequences rather than because of the moral and spiritual prescriptions disapproving such an action. While these physical and empirical factors may be guiding principles used by many to determine their behavior, they are derived from the moral and spiritual underlying reality. That is to say, every form of correct behavior in social, political or public life is derived from the law of God, which is written on the hearts of men. Of course, free will allows for the violation of God's law. The choice is ours.

Kant's use of logic can be applied to a more complex example — the fact that there is something rather than nothing. When I refer to nothing I mean absolute nothingness. I am not referring to nothing as physicists do. Their description entails objects which pop into existence seemingly out of nowhere. But this is simply a nowhere of pre-existence of which we are unaware — objects exist, but we don't know how or where they exist. The definition I use is absolute nothingness. The fact that there is something, logically leads to the conclusion that there always was something that did not have a cause, i.e. is non-contingent. The possibility of absolute nothingness is eliminated, because there would be nothing which existed to overcome nothingness.

Intellectually, this is a mind blowing thought to embrace, but logic demands it must be so. The force which exists must be infinitely powerful. From the Judeo-Christian tradition, we believe that entity is a personal God. That knowledge is known solely on the basis of Divine Revelation. For non-believers there is no notion of an all powerful, loving, personal Being, i.e. God. But for them, there is still the inexplicable mystery of how something always existed. Through logic, they have an intimation of the underlying truth we have from revelation.

Conscience

Since, I mentioned conscience, a word about that. Many far more intelligent and holier individuals than I have addressed this issue. I approach it from a slightly different angle, though I believe, in the end, we agree.

If conscience is, as I believe, the Word of God communicated to each individual, then we play no part in forming conscience; it stands on its own. What we form is our response to conscience. We must accept it as given, not as we would like it. It may disturb us, make us feel uncomfortable, offend our sensibilities, or in any number of ways present us with the truth we would rather not hear. This is God through Jesus, the Christ, speaking the truth to us. Our responsibility is to accept it without any editorial comment on our part. If we honestly receive the Word of God, then we are obligated to follow it. This will, on occasion, place us in a position of opposition to established behavior or practice. It is an uncomfortable and challenging position, but by no means unique and most likely necessary. Saints are made by following conscience — Thomas More for example. The Blessed Mother might not have accepted God's plan had she ignored her conscience. The difficulty is sublimating the self and surrendering to God. Knowing what is right, is a gift from God. We have free will and a stubborn nature. Forming the response to what we know is correct is where the difficulty lies. It is this formation that we work on all of our lives. And prayer is the key to correct formation.

My perspective on conscience is not based on some subjective quirk of mind. I view conscience as I do truth. Truth stands independent of what I may think about any particular reality. Its authenticity is completely autonomous. What I think does not affect the truth at all. I have the free will to say, "That is not my truth," but by doing so I deceive myself as well as others. We form neither truth nor conscience; we decide how we will respond to them. The Empire State Building is in New York City. I did not form that fact, but I can choose to believe it or not. Along with the commandment, conscience tells us stealing is a sin. I played no part in forming that word of God, but I can form my response to it. The more we eliminate pride, the clearer our vision becomes in forming the correct response to conscience.

We are surrounded by a world which imposes itself on us unceasingly with practical concerns. Those impositions can constrain us to shade conscience and truth to fit our needs. We should be aware of this pressure and guard against it. We constantly walk a tight rope.

Defense of Life

The respect for life extends well beyond the unborn; it includes the elderly, the infirm, the criminal on death row — in fact all the living in any category. The seventh commandment forbids murder, i.e. the intentional and premeditated killing of another. But to the extant we can, we ought to refrain from all killing.

Because of the imperfect world we live in there are exceptions, though they are very limited. It may become necessary to kill another human being in self-defense, or in a just war. In these cases, we would be guilty of killing, but not guilty of murder. And after such an incident our first inclination should be to express our sorrow to God and ask His forgiveness for an act which should never have occurred.

By inaction in the cases of self-defense, just war or a criminal on death row, we may sin by omission. In each case it would be best that no life would be taken; with self-defense, disarming or immobilizing an attacker would be preferred; in a just war, a mere demonstration of destruction would be preferable to actual mayhem and death; with death row, we would have to ensure that no one unjustly convicted would be put to death. The guilty, more appropriately, would be sentenced to life imprisonment. This of course is an ideal. While it is theoretically sound, in reality, the situation is messy. It is complicated by numerous factors, many of which are out of our control.

In a perfect world we would have no such problem but, as it is, we must deal with the situation as it exists. I find no cogent argument against killing to save oneself, or a family member, in a just war, or to prevent a greater evil from destroying one's country or civilization itself. We could conclude that killing should be eliminated in all cases, but then consideration must be given to the prospect that by doing so we allow evil to hold sway in the world. It is an alternative with ominous implications. With death row inmates there may be certain instances when the state is correct to exact the death penalty. Hopefully, such cases will become increasingly rare. The elimination of the death penalty may be preferred by many. But it is not likely to be universally adopted, the most basic reason being that human nature would have to change drastically. All impulses to commit the types of crimes which provoke the use of the death penalty would have to be eliminated. I don't foresee that happening any time soon, at least not before the second coming. To the extent of our capability, we should treat all life as sacred, i.e. authored by God. This certainly means no murder, and as far as killing, it should be avoided whenever possible. It is lamentable, but some problems cannot be resolved without violence. Even Satan and his angels had to be violently expelled from heaven. This is a complex subject and one in which, in a manner of speaking, we are trying to read the mind of God. Have I read it correctly? I am not bold enough to answer—I simply do not know. I can only follow my conscience in such thorny matters, hope I am correct and end each prayer as Padre Pio did: "Thy will be done." All life should be considered sacred, especially human life. Every human life should be vigorously defended. Abuse or murder can only occur when a person is objectified, that is perceived as on object rather than a human being.

Abortion

Abortion is the act of killing a living human being. All abortions are murderous, save perhaps in the case where the life of the mother is threatened. In that situation, we may have to rely on the conscience of the mother, or on the consciences of both parents. The choice is indeed difficult and one not easily decided. It requires much prayer for guidance. We will not be able to stop abortion completely, but what must be stopped is any and all government funding of abortion, either directly, indirectly or surreptitiously. We must teach our children and anyone else who is willing to listen, that life is sacred and that all life must be respected and protected. With the possible exception listed above, there is no valid defense of abortion. In all cases, without exception, abortion imposes the death sentence on a defenseless, innocent, living human being. It is a barbaric practice. Our responsibility is to defend life in the public square, to do it constantly, elegantly, with strength and courage, and to do it with respect for those who disagree with us. For they are our sisters and brothers also; we should pray for them so their eyes, ears and hearts are opened to the truth. We should pray for each other, so that we do not fear to speak out in the public square. And we should hold our leaders, whether in the public or religious arena, accountable. They must be in the forefront along with us in this effort. The effort itself cannot be forced on anyone; it is a position which must become self-evident to each individual. It is necessary to continually teach and promote the fact that all life is sacred. If we fall silent, or become lax in preserving and promoting this truth, it will be eroded. Value cannot be preserved without effort. Thus history teaches and thus we have cause to be vigilant. If we hope to preserve and see the continuance of sacred values in the generations to come, diligent and constant attention is necessary.

I have observed that both clergy and lay people have been lax in defense of life. Among some this condition still persists. We, the lay people, have been operating on the premise that the authorities in the clergy, at all levels, are constantly and actively addressing the evils of abortion. To a large extent we have been in error. We must be actively engaged in promoting life, in cooperation with the clergy when possible and independently when necessary. We cannot simply assume the authorities will act responsibly. In my experience, the most profound efforts to combat abortion have come from the laity, not the clergy. In the fight against abortion, not all can march, or contribute money, or write with influence in the public arena. But we all have the ability to demonstrate that we stand for the sanctity of life with the way we live our lives in this secular society according to the laws of God. We do this with every gesture and interaction we have with every person we meet. Loving those we disagree with, and practically demonstrating it, has an immense effect on listeners' willingness to engage in arguments which would otherwise be rejected outright. Those who champion abortion are not so readily persuaded by words or even by marches per se, but they do take pause when they see a high quality of life, i.e. when they unknowingly see the acceptance of God's life in our own.

Some of the clergy, at all levels and for a variety of reasons, have avoided addressing the evils of abortion. Much of it has to do with offending sensibilities or potentially losing membership, thus diminishing revenue. If the truth offends, perhaps it should. Being made aware of a flaw, we should be glad of the knowledge and be about the business of correcting it. We should not burn the prophets—they were commissioned by God to correct problems. Pastors are under pressure to keep their parishes fiscally sound. By not addressing sensitive issues directly, everyone stays complacent and the revenue stream remains safe. But is that what the Church is? Is it a financially stable organization, or is it a spiritual organization? Can both be achieved? These are topics which are rarely addressed and discussed. They should be, even though they are difficult. Seeing deficiencies in the church, our efforts need to be focused on correction, not on tearing down.

In the political arena, there are issues about which all but the incompetent agree. But even in such cases, one side or the other will take the opposing view, not because they know or believe it to be true, but for sheer political advantage. Abortion is one of those issues. In my opinion, I believe it is accurate to say that most Catholic politicians who favor abortion do so for political advantage. They know the practice is barbaric and that it is the destruction of human life. I have never heard any proponent of abortion say: "I wish my parents or parent had decided to abort me." Until the proponents can honestly say this, and attempt to defend the proposition, they demonstrate their inability to address the issue in an honest polemic. But their game is power, and the desire to achieve and hold on to power trumps every other consideration. It is why we must be constantly on the attack. We must attack with every weapon at our disposal—not opponents personally but rather the vile and inhuman practice itself. In all things, we judge not our fellows, but we do evaluate actions and behavior. And we sin by omission if we fail to affirm what we have been taught, and fail to call out error. Every Democratic candidate running for the presidency in 2020 and the leaders of the party support abortion under all circumstances. Gone is the once voiced position that abortion should be rare. The position now asserts that abortion should be the norm even to the point of infanticide. They have become assassins. I do not condemn them. I do not judge them. I evaluate their behavior. I find it lacking in grace and an affront to human dignity. It is also a violation of the law of God, but in our pluralistic society that carries little weight, even among Catholics. On this issue, Democratic candidates and the leadership of the party have managed to divorce themselves from most Democratic voters. Most human beings, political affiliation notwithstanding, are not in favor of infanticide.

The only conclusion which can be drawn about such a drastic advocacy for abortion is beyond political advantage: it is the practice of evil. We are a nation of great intestinal strength throughout the land, but issues such as this one must be addressed and corrected with alacrity. We are not capable of enduring attacks on our integrity, vicious as they might be, for very long before disastrous results are felt. I have always been taught that if this nation falls, it will fall from within. There is corruption at high levels, and it must be countered. If America falls, there will be no other place on earth to run for protection.

The Declaration of Independence begins with, "We the People," and if we find leaders in government, the clergy, industry and the media who are corrupt, we the people are duty bound to correct that situation. If we fail to do so, it is at our peril. We should not forget that when the founders set in motion the division of power between the executive, legislative and judicial branches of the government, they added a fourth leg to the mix: the power of the people. That is a gift; it should not be abused, but used judiciously when necessary.

Marriage

Marriage is the union of one man and one woman. No other arrangement—whether singular, among two or more individuals, an individual and an animal or an individual and an inanimate object—is a marriage. Any pronouncement to the contrary, from any human source, is error. In this world and society, any combination is possible due to freedom, but no other combination is a marriage, no matter what anyone says to the contrary. I disagree with the current vogue for "gay marriage;" I do not believe that such a thing exists. The secular society will of course champion the practice. And even among some of the clergy of all faiths this error is falsely taught. In a free society, individuals have the right to form any relationship they choose. What they do not have is the authority over the definition of terms based on whims, false premises or emotional need. Neither do they have the authority to force their opinions on the society at large. There is no room for hatred or discrimination of those who follow a path other than the traditional and biblical view of marriage. But those of us who hold that position have every right to disagree with any other definition of marriage without recrimination, without being labeled bigots and without being forced into accepting definitions we know to be false. The law allows one to choose the arrangement desired. It does not grant the right or authority to change the definition of marriage or to force said definition on the society at large, much less to compel its acceptance. While we have the right to disagree with the term "gay marriage," (finding the two words to be mutually exclusive) we do not have the right to force our beliefs on anyone. Those of us who know that marriage is between one man and one woman have no desire to offend, deride or criticize anyone. The problem lies with the condition and the practice. Respectfully, we cannot accept a completely flawed definition of marriage. But because we disagree, it does not mean we hate. When a teacher tells a student they have spelled a word wrong, it is done to help the student improve—not because the teacher hates the student. The objections to new definitions of marriage are based on deeply held religious convictions, logic and human tradition. They have nothing to do with hatred or prejudice. Hatred and prejudice are certainly part of human behavior, but to ascribe them as the reasons for any and all dissenting opinions is a grave error.

Currently, it has become the position of some members of the clergy in the Catholic Church that "gay marriage" is equal to heterosexual marriage. They teach that God created "gay" individuals, so they must be good as they are and have no need to change. This kind of thinking and proffering is, of course, contrary to scripture and negates the Law of God. It could not be further from the truth and is both dangerous and damaging. By logical extension all that exists was created by God; therefore, all things are good and there is no need for anything or anyone to change. In this philosophy since God created murderers they are good as they are and have no need of change. Even in a totally secular society that is an absurd notion. Simply because information is coming from an authority figure—some "expert"—or is presented in a sophisticated and highly intelligent manner we must still be on guard. Teachings of this misguided type will succeed in driving more members out of the church. It seems the aegis for this thinking springs from a misguided view of acceptance and mercy. Jesus healed, but followed the healing by saying, "Go and sin no more." Promulgating false doctrine benefits no one. We are commanded not to judge. We are also commanded to profess and defend what is true.

● ● ●

You have probably noticed that the wind has started to increase in intensity and the sea is quite agitated. The forecast is less than favorable; we press onward with vigor.

Gender

With absolute clarity we can state that there are, in fact, only two sexes: male and female. All other terms to designate a gender type other than the aforementioned are in the same category as gay marriage—nonexistent. It has become culturally acceptable to champion a variety of transgender categories, feel as though you are female one day and male another day and advocate for LGBT families. Even among established religions, members of the clergy, including "Catholic" clergy, will advocate for these positions. These advocates are quick to say, "God embraces all sinners and so should the church." I agree; the statement is correct. What is missing is a clear understanding of what it means.

God calls all of us no matter what our sins. But God calls us out of our sins into His just, merciful, loving embrace. He does not call us to stay in our sins, accepting that we will continue in our ways. He calls us to discard our ways, and accept His ways. Religion is a practical enterprise. To paraphrase St. Augustine, when we discover we are capable of change, we are obligated to change for the good. Intimating or teaching that we are incapable of change is both morally bankrupt and logically flawed.

I dare say all of us think of education as a practical necessity. Who would conclude that educators were doing a good job if at the end of the education process the students remained in the same place that they were in when they entered kindergarten! They are called to change, not to remain the same. They are called from a position of deficiency to one in which they acquire information, knowledge and wisdom. If any clergy teach that God or the Church accepts all sinners as they are, with need no need to change, they are nothing short of disingenuous. And they are false teachers.

We see many abnormalities in the world. They can be physical, mental, emotional, or psychological. They occur due to accidents, or errors in nature. A blind, deaf, physically or mentally handicapped individual is not abnormal, but the condition they suffer is abnormal. We don't discriminate, or dehumanize or look down on any of these people; we simply recognize the problem they have. To deny there is a problem in such cases flies in the face of logic and reason. It distorts truth.

There is no difference when it concerns matters "gay." We are not discriminating, or hating or practicing prejudice. We are simply stating the truth: these good people are suffering from an abnormal condition. They, as with all who are afflicted, must acknowledge it. It is no shame to acknowledge that one is blind or deaf. Neither is it a shame to acknowledge that one has a proclivity towards homosexuality. The problem is an unwillingness to acknowledge that the condition is an abnormality, and to equate it with a condition where the deficiency does not exist. The scripture is clear: members of the same sex engaging in sexual intercourse are sinning just as heterosexuals who are adulterers also sin. Scripture calls us to be perfect.

If the culture is willing to accept that a male can at any time declare he feels like a female and therefore can enter a women's bathroom or a girl's locker room, then it will also accept that a non-musician who has never played the violin can, at any time, declare that he or she feels they are a concert violinist and must be allowed to play the Beethoven violin concerto with the Boston Symphony Orchestra. And if denied, the non-musician can accuse the deniers of practicing discrimination. We are not discriminating against the homosexual community. We recognize their talents, abilities and rights. We also recognize that they suffer from an abnormal condition.

● ● ●

Lightning strikes surround the vessel. The waves increase in ferocity. The wind gains power. What conditions will we experience in the foreseeable future?

THAT WHICH MATTERS

Family

No human organization, association or enterprise is more important or essential than the family. It is the unit on which civilization is built. The direct results of family breakdown include damaged, flawed or completely impoverished aspects of a well-functioning culture. An avalanche of societal problems ensue:

- Poor education;
- High rates of crime;
- An increased reliance on drugs and alcohol;
- Corruption in business and government;
- An increase in poverty;
- An increase in personal stress;
- The breakdown of civility; and
- A sense of isolation.

These are among the worse of the effects on the society at large. The individual is the basic building block of every institution in a society. The family is the unit which produces the individual; get the individual right, and institutions will flourish.

One does not have to be religious to appreciate the critical role of the family. But those of us who are religious understand that the notion of family comes from God. In Scripture we read "Let us make man in our image." See God says "Let us...," not "Let me..." We may therefore think of God as a family. And God shares that uniting element with us in the creation of man and woman. Because we have free will, we either work building the family or work tearing it down. And as the family goes, so goes the civilization. The position which I take, (i.e. that without belief in God, building family is impossible) will be disputed. A word of explanation about what I mean.

There are obviously examples of individual families who are beautifully formed without belief in God. These are the exception to the rule. And there is no guarantee that the strong family association will continue from generation to generation. The basis of values not rooted in God is strictly human and changeable over time. Without a belief that there is an unalterable standard, i.e. the Law of God, there is no fixed point from which to deviate. For those who do not acknowledge an unalterable standard, any imaginable behavior is possible and equal to any other imaginable behavior. This leads to a distorted approach to life.

For most families, without a fixed standard, anything goes. Examples: High rates of divorce; high rates of single motherhood; high rates of births outside of marriage; high incidents of men who feel they can impregnate women and walk away with no sense of responsibility. The plethora of these assaults on the family and their practical effect is an economic and cultural disaster for the women, their children, and for the society in general. I acknowledge that, among those who profess to believe in God, deviation from the ideal also occurs. They must be vigilant. But there is a difference. That difference is based on the foundation of our values, and how we determine that foundation. I see two related but different paradigms: Ethics and morality.

While ethics and morality can be related, it is not always the case. Ethics is based on human norms. When those norms are of a high and noble standard they may coincide with morality. But human norms are subject to indiscriminate change—they can be completely subjective in nature. When this occurs they may take a drastic turn away from morality. Among the religious, morality is revealed by God, and is unchangeable. It is not subject to cultural bias or fad and is not subject to becoming outdated. It may not be followed as it should be but it remains fixed, immutable and objectively true because it issues from God. This of course provides no evidence for those who do not believe in God. For them the laws of morality are just one of a number of human opinions about how we should conduct ourselves.

If we select morality as the foundation upon which we base our behavior, at the very least we have an accurate standard by which to measure. One may fall short of the standard, but that does not diminish the standard; it merely reflects some lack in the individual. It eliminates a convenient excuse: "The fault was something or someone else's, but not mine." Since ethics are subject to change, this convenient excuse is always available. It allows for no limits or boundaries. Because we determine the strictures of the ethics, we can change them as soon as they become inconvenient, and thus there are no limits on our behavior. This seems like freedom, but in fact it is license. License would be subject to this unlimited freedom, and therefore subject to be misused. To be sure there are those who profess belief in God yet break the moral law knowingly. And many who do not believe in God yet keep a strict ethical code, unknowingly keep the word of God. I cannot speak for God, but it may well be that He will judge us by our actions, and not by labels or beliefs.

What has this to do with families? Everything.

The word of God is the foundation of the family, the culture, the civilization, the nation and the world. The stronger the belief in a moral code outside of ourselves that we are bound to, the stronger every facet of family life will be. Enhanced are love, devotion, charity, happiness, work, the wisdom to handle success and the grace and strength to deal with failure and sorrow — and for some, dealing with the horror that life sometimes presents.

Every family seeks security. We work for food, clothing and shelter as basics and seek, through education, to advance careers and acquire any number of possessions and positions of prominence. This is all good. What is added by the moral code is the knowledge that all of this is temporary and will disappear. What will remain is something much more important: How we managed those finite aspects of life and how we treated our fellow man. That will go with us into eternity when we will stand before God and give an accounting. And on this earth it provides us with the ability to build great nations and maintain them. Observe any nation around our world: If the government is oppressive or malfunctioning in some way, look to the strength of the family. The more dysfunctional the family, the more dysfunctional the government will be. A poor government cannot long endure in a nation of well-formed families. Well-formed families provide well-formed individuals for business, industry and government. This constant flow of positive energy, though not fool proof, will normally produce a well functioning government. Dysfunctional family members, constantly in the flow, will have the opposite effect. While families are not the only cause of well functioning or poorly functioning government, they certainly play an important role.

What we experience in our country is a type of equilibrium. We have both functional and dysfunctional families, and this is reflected in the way the government operates. To this point in our history the functional families have carried the day. Whether that will remain so is the challenge we face.

It is certain that we will not be able to be completely successful with every family and families will not be completely successful with each individual. But a concerted striving toward excellence will produce fruitful results. Secularists know that we are, as they would characterize it, subject to bad habits or character flaws. Those of us who are religious know we are subject to temptation and fall into sin.

We know we must be constantly on guard against influences which have the potential to destroy. We will not create perfection, nor will we achieve Utopia; we can, however, continually improve even if extremely slowly.

Friendship

One of the finest and most wholesome associations humans have established is friendship. It begins without demands of the other and flowers to the point where all demands are self-imposed to the benefit of the other. A true friendship develops into true love. The kind of love St. Paul (Saul) writes about. Because technology can easily allow individuals to isolate themselves, friendship is under more assault than at any time in history. Because of the instant gratification provided by cell phones and iPads (without effort or commitment!) one can be in the company of others, yet ignore them and be completely isolated. Aspects of this are readily observed. The technical devices around us should be used as tools, not as substitutes for human interaction. The great danger presented is that immersion in technology may lead to viewing individuals as impersonal. Seeing people as objects is an evil we have experienced in the past and see before us now in the new pro-abortion laws passed in several states. It is an evil we ought not broach and need to expunge as soon as it rears its ugly head.

Failure & Success

Of these two, I would caution that success is far more dangerous than failure. While failure has the potential to — and sometimes does — crush an individual, most often, after an initial low, it will energize and spur a renewed urge to succeed. In many cases, failure is the direct cause of success. Failures along the way will often ensure that success does not spoil the individual. It may well be that without the occasional failure, one is more susceptible to being spoiled by success.

Success has the potential of posing a danger to everyone. Why? Because it tends to allow the individual to take for granted what has been accomplished, ignore or abandon the very practices which have made one successful or become lazy or complaisant. The dangers of success are on constant display in our country, obvious to even the most casual observer. Throughout the print and broadcast media, in entertainment, in education, in politics, in our houses of worship, and in the general culture, we see what I call the dumbed-down syndrome, i.e. the attempt on the part of organizations or individuals to water down standards toward mediocrity rather than elevating them to the highest degree possible. In a misplaced attempt to be inclusive, merciful or all encompassing, standards can be lowered, definitions changed, mores revised, history distorted, etc., all done in the name of progress and all growing out of a desire for easy success for all. Success can easily lead to mediocrity. It is difficult to spoil failure but quite easy to spoil success — the field is ripe and vulnerable. The temptation to take the path of least resistance, in the sense of lowering requirements, performance standards and the definition of achievement, must itself be resisted. These types of operations will produce a false sense of success which will only complicate the problem. The ingredients of success (e.g. hard work, dedication, time, natural talent) should not be forgotten, ignored or misused. The danger is in dismissing these contributors to success as trifles. Problems creep in silently, almost unnoticed, and the process is relentless. It affects all institutions and aspects of life. The urge to be admired, to receive benefits, to be part of the crowd, to get along with everyone, also plays a part. None are immune.

> It is difficult to spoil failure but quite easy to spoil success.

Perhaps using the term "pop culture" is not the best way to describe what ensnares us; "zeitgeist" may be more apt. The zeitgeist is that feeling of comfort which allows a foul breeze to push us in a direction better not taken. The liberal powers in the entertainment industry and media railed about the "violence" portrayed in the westerns made in the thirties, forties and fifties. Then that very entertainment industry proceeded to give the public more graphic violence on screen than viewers could ever have imagined, making the violence portrayed in the old westerns look like child's play by comparison. And the press? They celebrated the end of minimal violence and embraced the graphic violence with open arms, transferring the blame from the industry and themselves to the public, insisting that it was what the public demanded, when in fact it was what the industry supplied.

The industry did the same with the portrayal of sex and use of vulgar language. Easy success has led to complacency. The lure of wealth has led producers to provide material which appeals to consumers' basest instincts rather than that which is of high quality. There are some excellent movies, but they are not normally the money makers and are definitely in the minority.

This appeal to the lowest common denominator is detrimental to the progress of a society; it keeps people in place at best and most often leads to decline. The old aphorism, "buyer beware," should be kept in mind. Small groups of the elite—the best and brightest among us in government, industry, entertainment and churches—wield great influence. We respect their brilliance and achievements and tend to be guided by them. We become reluctant to question them because of that respect. There is danger in this. They can and often do go astray as easily and frequently as anyone else. When they do, because of the power and influence they hold, the results often prove to be disastrous. History provides us with many examples. Great intelligence is not always coupled with common sense and wisdom. Intelligence without these qualities can cause great damage. Common sense is disparaged these days, but one should remember what the poet William Blake said about it: "An uncommon amount of common sense is genius."

As individuals we have the responsibility of being mindful of what we are being fed. If the authorities are not interested in raising standards, it becomes our duty to do so. Too much comfort and success tend to diminish the desire to excel. While not true of all, in most cases the majority will follow the path of least resistance. Success comes from God given talent, to which we add hard work and dedication. There are no short cuts — at least none not fraught with great danger.

The antidote for being spoiled by success is to develop a strong character and powerful interior life. The surest way of accomplishing this is to adhere to the law of God. Doing so allows the mind to focus on eternal truth rather than on the mundane and merely personal.

> "An uncommon amount of common sense is genius."
>
> William Blake

GOVERNMENT

The best form of Government is a benevolent dictatorship. The caveat is that only one version of this is acceptable, namely, one where God is in charge. Since we do not know exactly when that will occur, we have the next best form of government—a democratic republic. The United States of America, with all of its messiness, is the prime example. We are certainly not without fault but have, since our inception, managed to create a better life for our own citizens and for millions throughout the world—more so than any other nation which has ever existed. Since 1776 we have been constantly working to perfect ourselves. The process fluctuates up and down, but the general trend has been, and continues to be, toward the improvement of our country, society and culture. The saddest and most traumatizing event in our history was the Civil War. It divided our people and the divide lingers with us. Had we been able to resolve the issues that provoked that war through peaceful means, much else in our history may have been different.

We grapple with the same problem which occupied the minds of the founders. How much control do we want the Federal Government to have over the institutions in our nation? Striking the correct balance is the challenge we face. Aware that the Government, private individuals and institutions are subject to the same faulty judgments, abuses of power and corruption, we move forward trying to create a more perfect union. Many of the leaders of the two major political parties are far less aligned with this movement forward than the citizens they supposedly represent. A well informed electorate is critical to a properly functioning democratic government. There are benefits as well as drawbacks to the easy dissemination of information we experience. It allows for a great deal of misinformation to spread rapidly. We must be cognizant of this and guard against it. On the positive side, it allows us to understand and identify officials in the Government or Church who stray from principle. We are then capable of demanding reform.

The government in the U.S. has been successful because of the separation of powers. The founders realized that everyone and every organization require a watch dog. Without oversight we invite any number of abuses. Human society will never eliminate abuses completely, but we have a system in place which minimizes them as far as possible.

The U.S. Constitution and the Establishment Clause

As stated: "Congress shall make no law respecting an establishment of religion, or prohibiting the free exercise thereof." The Amendment goes on to guarantee freedom of the press, speech and peaceable assembly. The first Amendment does not call for the separation of Church and State: It prohibits the establishment of a state sponsored religion. Great wisdom from the founders...in fact Solomon-like. The notion of a separation of Church and State is a false argument unworthy of consideration. The Government and its agents should not be preventing, as they often do, the free exercise of religion. That free exercise extends out of the houses of worship into the public square. The government has no right or authority to prevent religious symbols from being displayed on private or public property. The display of religious symbols anyplace on private or public property is an exercise of freedom; it does not imply, suggest or in any other way assert that the government has established a religion of any kind. To suggest the opposite is absurd. Even more inane is the notion that a single atheist can have a religious symbol removed from public property because he or she finds it personally offensive. I find it personally offensive that pornography is on sale in public places. Do I therefore have the right to demand that all such sales must stop immediately and, if not, all establishments offering such material be forcibly closed? That would be absurd. Every several minutes some new personal offense would have to be addressed. It seems that intolerance is widely condemned unless, of course, it concerns religious matters. The faith communities in our country and their spokespeople, the clergy, have neglected to address this issue properly. What is there to fear? The U S. Constitution is on our side. I am a single voice with no influence or power and can be ignored. Those in positions of authority have the power and the responsibility to demand that the First Amendment be adhered to as written. It is well beyond the time to reject imaginary restrictions on religious freedom no matter how cleverly argued. It is disappointing to hear even those who are in favor of religious liberty using the phrase "separation of church and state." The quote comes from a letter written by Thomas Jefferson to the Danbury Baptist Association in 1802. It is nowhere found in the Constitution but is seized upon by those who eschew any notion of religion. The idea that the constitution requires a separation of church and state should be countered at every opportunity, and most certainly by not clothing Jefferson's phrase with Constitutional authority.

There is another currently popular discussion about the Constitution which evaluates it as being outdated and in need of change. The Constitution along with the Declaration of Independence has served the country well, and continues to do so. As required, amendments can be added; it has been happening since 1791, when the first 10 amendments were added. Amendments eleven through twenty-seven have been added in a continuing process from 1795 through 1992. To argue that these documents are outdated, and need to be completely changed ignores history. The Declaration makes reference to God at least four times, and the principles guiding both documents find their source in the Judeo-Christian tradition. The truths found there are unchangeable and perfect. They are a major reason for the great success and progress made in so many areas that are so vitally important to the people of the United States and the world. Success is not easily achieved, but it can be easily lost. If we allow ourselves to be influenced by cultures and philosophies which have failed, and abandon the principles which have guided us to success, then we too will fail. Radical secularists advocate, and would welcome, the disappearance of religion from the culture. What they do not realize is that by eliminating religion, a great many other ingredients which have made us successful would disappear also. And their attempt to create what, in their minds, is a better and greater society, would ultimately lead to its demise. There is no doubt that we must resist this type of change with intelligence and kindness, but also with strength. Before our eyes we have the example of the missteps taken by the Catholic Church after Vatican II. Pope John the XXIII's intent was to open the windows and doors to let in fresh air (aggiornamento). In many ways, the opposite occurred. Those who were liberal-minded among the clergy and laity hijacked the Pope's intent and changed the direction in which the church was headed. The Church jettisoned many aspects which attracted, formed and nurtured faithful followers — followers who led fulfilling lives and saw death as returning to their Father in Heaven. It replaced glorious ritual, music, architecture and other fundamentals with the common and mundane. It succeeded in keeping the congregation in place rather than lifting them up to God. Many of the troubles the Church is currently experiencing have as their source the aftermath of Vatican II. It is all too easy to misstep and let down one's guard. We must always keep in mind that evil never rests, nor does it discriminate; it is equally happy destroying an individual, a culture, a government, a nation or a religion. If we forget this we are at sea without a rudder. The founders were not perfect, but they realized that human rights are God given, not government given. The founding documents loudly and proudly proclaim this. We should neither forget nor dismiss this truth from the public forum.

Military Service

This idea will meet with opposition from everyone except former military and those who are currently serving. Every male in the United States should serve in the military; females can serve if they choose to do so. The term should be three years, and one of those should be overseas. Those whose draft status is 4-F (i.e. not suitable for military service due to health) can serve in administrative or support jobs. Only those who suffer from severe physical or mental disabilities should be exempt. There may be other reasons for exemption and they should be determined judiciously.

Serving one's country should be considered an honor. It would instill a sense of appreciation for the country, which is currently lacking among many of our young people. Knowledge of how a large portion of the rest of the earth operates would open the eyes of many. The Service would produce better citizens who would be committed to their country. Many young people have a negative view of America; it is an attitude which reveals them as being arrested in adolescence. Service in the armed forces would help to transform such a view into something much more realistic. Due to the fact that the subject of history has been eliminated from the curriculum, many young people have either a distorted knowledge of U.S. history or no knowledge of it at all. Their views are based on disinformation supplied by a variety of sources, from the media to the internet. Service in the military would ground them in reality. All would participate in carrying the burden of securing freedom and providing for peace. In our past history (Revolutionary War, Civil War, WW I and WW II) all segments of the society served. The rich and poor, the educated and uneducated, the lowly and the mighty all felt the need to serve. And in all segments of society were those who found a way to avoid service. But they were in the minority. What is more, the ability to use the loop-holes only works if tolerated. We should return to the draft for all males who are able to serve.

Immigration

Every country has the right to set its immigration policy. Without an immigration policy, one of the essential ingredients in preserving the integrity and ethos of a nation state is placed in jeopardy. Indifference as to whom is coming into the country has the potential of causing both physical and cultural harm. Immigration policy in the U.S. has been manipulated to work against the best interests of our citizens, take advantage of those coming here illegally and treating unfairly those who have come here legally.

Does anyone want to leave their homeland unless forced to for some reason? I don't think so. There are legitimate reasons for emigrating to another country—that is not disputed. But every nation has the right to determine who and how many immigrants it will allow to enter at any given time. Considerations involved are many—moral, economic, practical and legal among them.

Responsibilities rest on both sides. As the nation accepting immigrants, we should know who they are and that we can offer a situation in which they can succeed. To bring immigrants in and immediately make them dependent damages both them and the nation. We have a great deal of domestic poverty; it makes no sense to create more of what we currently don't handle properly. We currently have a legal immigration policy which allows approximately 1 million immigrants into the country yearly (675,000 legal immigrants plus their children and family members). If that policy needs certain changes they should be made. But illegal immigration should be stopped.

Immigrants should want to become citizens of the U.S., learn the English language, study our history, appreciate our religious foundation and adopt our laws and customs. This serves to benefit everyone and ensures the strength of the country. It would be counterproductive, illogical, destructive, and completely without merit to allow immigrants into the country who have the express desire to transform our country and traditions into what they have just fled. Those with an ideology which insists that they must transform us as soon as they possibly can need not come and we need not invite them. We would be allowing them to destroy our freedom, which has been won at a high price. And at the same time, those immigrants would be working to destroy the very freedom they came here to enjoy. This applies to communists and members of any other fringe group which would seek to undermine the principles on which the country was founded and operates.

There are dishonest arguments on both sides of this issue. I will address two of the most egregious.

One economic argument is that illegal immigrants provide cheap labor. That is true. A second economic reality is that a citizen is deprived of a job, possibly at a higher wage. And the illegal immigrant is taken advantage of because the pay received is well below what it should be. The profit motive is at work—profit at the expense of both citizen and illegal. There is certainly an ethical and moral problem here. The moral problem is shared with those who would completely ban immigrants who are poor, uneducated or disadvantaged. These are not criteria on which allowing entrance to immigrants should be based.

What must be determined is the number of immigrants we can take—what is sustainable? And they must be legal immigrants. Some immigrants may come with skills which allow them to be self-sufficient immediately, but many will not. Many will have to be supported, at least for some time, and none of the officials advocating unfettered immigration will bear the personal burden of supporting any of them. That task will fall to U.S. citizens, civic organizations and religious organizations. Almost never is the question raised about why the governments in the countries these people are fleeing operate so terribly. And further, why is there so little effort expended to change that situation? Officials in this country, using other peoples' money and resources, pass the problems on to the general public, or certain segments of the general population, and never experience any of the problems they create.

Individuals in government and other institutions—including religious organizations—advocating an open border policy should experience, first- hand and personally, the work involved in absorbing all the immigrants they so casually transfer to the general public care. Rather than a nice and tidy theory which looks perfect on paper, they might gain valuable insights into the actual practical consequences of what they advocate by having to confront the problem directly. Immigrants have brought with them their best qualities, which have influenced and enriched our culture, and at the same time they have sought to adopt America's best qualities. Immigration is an important ingredient which has helped to make this nation so successful for so many.

Very rarely is the root cause of the immigration problem addressed. Little attention is given to the fact that incompetent or repressive government policies cause people to flee their own home lands. U.S. Government officials who see and try to address these problems are often attacked on the grounds that they are interfering in the internal affairs of another sovereign nation. Consequently, relief for millions who suffer under repressive governments does not come. While acknowledging this is a complex problem, an international effort should be mounted to confront rogue governments through diplomatic and economic means. This would certainly require an enormous commitment, but a concerted effort to do so on the part of the democratic nations around the globe, would be a good first step leading to an eventual solution. Almost never do we hear that the conditions forcing people to reluctantly leave their countries should be changed. In the most repressive countries, people leave only if fortunate enough to escape. History teaches it is better to address a threat or problem in its early stages rather than waiting until it develops to the point requiring a response which has catastrophic consequences.

The United States cannot solve all the problems in the world, but it can create a just immigration system for itself. It can initiate an effort in the Americas to improve the lives of the people of Central and South America by applying maximum pressure on renegade governments and corrupt dictators. This can only be accomplished with the efforts and cooperation of the citizens of the subject nations; without their full participation, we will not be successful. We should be very reluctant to intervene militarily as the results are often counter-productive. In the interim, all immigration into this country must be legal, and if that means securing the entire southern border, including a wall where practical, it should be done.

Capitalism

Capitalism, though not perfect, is exponentially superior to socialism or any other economic "...ism." Capitalism has done more to improve conditions for people throughout the world — regardless of race, color, religion or any other factor — than any other economic system. No other way of organizing an economy comes within light years of delivering the benefits Capitalism has yielded. It is a system which relies on, and profits from, the integrity and work ethic of all sectors of a society — individuals, private institutions, and public institutions.

The extent to which a high moral standard is operative in a society will determine the success of Capitalism therein. Because Capitalism must operate in a free society in order to succeed, it invites scrutiny. Thus, a watch dog is always necessary, whether the one being watched is an individual, a private institution or government agency. A watchdog cannot guarantee a perfectly running system, but it can usually stave off disastrous results.

A watchdog cannot guarantee a perfectly running system, but it can usually stave off disastrous results.

Capitalism allows for freedom in the market place: A free and open market based on competition is far superior to a market artificially controlled by a government. In the latter case, a small cadre of individuals control decision making, usually in their own self-interest. A Capitalist free market system spreads decision making over a wide population, encouraging creativity and innovation. In a free society, it is the paradigm providing the best route to educational and financial success—in other words, allowing all its citizens to thrive.

Unbridled Capitalism is nothing short of a disaster. Capitalism can often be perverted in legitimate democracies because, as with all things human, they are not perfect. This perverse form is often referred to as crony capitalism. It has been practiced around the world since the beginning of civilization, always with disastrous results: Those commanding the power live lives of conspicuous consumption, while the majority of citizens languish in desperate straits.

Crony Capitalism functions well under socialist and communist regimes. Both Socialism and Communism operate in oppressive environments where no scrutiny is allowed. These government controlled systems will inevitably fail, their basic flaw being the lack of accountability. Some form of scrutiny is always needed to limit abuses.

Health Care

Is health care a benefit to be privately pursued, or a fundamental human right which, under any and all circumstances, must be provided by either the government or private sector? I would like to preface my remarks by saying that I consider this a thorny issue. In order to address both the practical and moral aspects of the problem, I must digress for a moment.

In the Declaration of Independence, the framers expressed the idea that Life, Liberty and the pursuit of Happiness are among the rights with which all men are endowed by God. (This was perfectly clear to them!) They further declared that men institute governments to secure those rights. The men who espoused this were not members of the clergy, but they certainly got it right. And it is the direct result of being steeped in the Judeo/Christian tradition which led them to this conclusion. They correctly realized that rights come from God, not from governments; governments only have the power to secure or deny those rights.

Many questions arise with regard to healthcare, but these three come to my mind:

1. What is the role of the government? In my view, government should act as monitor ensuring that the established system, when implemented, runs equitably; it should not under any circumstances control the health care system. It should be a referee.

2. What is the role of the private sector? I recommend that the entire system should be developed in the private sector.

3. Is health care a right to be pursued or one which, under any and all circumstances, must be provided by either the government of private sector? Since, as I said above, the government would not run health care, it would have no role in providing any services.

I believe the private sector should and must provide health care for those in desperate need. This would include the mentally ill, those too poor to afford health insurance, and the disabled who cannot work. It would not include those who can afford health insurance but opt not to buy insurance.

One further question: Should the option of not participating in an established system be allowed? In my view the answer should be no. The best way of insuring that all who are able would participate would have to be determined in some fair and equitable fashion.

Now the disclaimer: I am not a doctor or other health care professional. I do not work in the pharmaceutical industry, in the medical insurance industry or as an administrator directing or managing a health care facility. I am one who lives under the presently functioning system, observes it carefully, and makes the observations and reflections given herein. I readily concede that it will take the contributions of many knowledgeable people from all sectors of the society to produce the best health care system possible.

If we are going to speak about health care as being a right, it then correctly falls under the categories of life, liberty and the pursuit of happiness. It is a right secured by individuals functioning with moral and civil responsibility. In addition to having a strong moral well spring, it should have the strong support of the Church and the Government.

No matter what solution we find to correct the faults in the current system, a nonpartisan accountability watchdog is absolutely necessary. The Federal Government is the best candidate for this role. The benefits are many, among them: The fact that the government is powerful, and can be an effective enforcer ensuring that all parties behave; it allows the private sector to develop and run the health care system; and, most importantly, it eliminates the Government as the sole power controlling the health care system. I am always worried about the Government having too much power. It would be especially worrisome if the Federal Government totally controlled health care. The watch dog would be eliminated, for whom, or what, in the private sector could effectively hold the Government accountable for misdeeds? The private sector is certainly capable of mischief; how much more so the Government? It has the unequalled power to either be a great monitor or a great manipulator. I prefer to see it in the former role.

Another word about too much power residing in one place: We are all aware that political retribution is a common practice in both political parties. When it comes to members of the House of Representatives or Senate, the political party with which they are affiliated will, when necessary, use every weapon at its disposal to ensure enactment of all of its policies. Consequences are incurred for non-compliance. The same unbridled lust for control would pertain if the Federal Government controlled health care. Instead of being a watchdog, ensuring that the private sector would not unfairly maltreat subscribers, the Government would be in a perfect position to do exactly that. There would no longer be an agent providing help or adjudication. The agency would no longer exist as a watchdog; in its place would be the most powerful agent, having at its disposal a variety of sophisticated and nuanced methods, allowing it to punish anyone it perceived as a political enemy. And all of this could be accomplished, ostensibly and innocently under the guise of bureaucracy.

If we can agree that the Federal Government should not run health care, we can then allow it to be constructed in the private sector. Patients, doctors and other health care professionals, religious leaders, insurance companies, with the support of government officials, should resolve to restructure and improve our health care system. The private sector should run health care. When the Government passed the Affordable Care Act, it affected the entire health care system. It would have been much more successful, and most probably would have attracted bipartisan support, if it had addressed the approximately 20 percent of the population who were in need of help. Perhaps the 20% figure is accurate, but it may not be. I am suspicious of all statistical information, including information which would support my positions. Some research states that the 20% figure includes 12.2% of all adults who were without insurance. Other research states that the percentage of the nonelderly uninsured was 17.1% in 2008; it then rose to 17.8% in 2010, and has declined since to 10.4% in 2018. Other research offers higher percentages. I do not have the resources to confirm the accuracy of any of the research. My point is this: win or lose the debate, I want my position to be based on fact and truth, not opinion.

For arguments sake, I will assume the percentage of the population uninsured before the Affordable Care Act was 50%. My position was and continues to be that it would have been more appropriate to correct one half of the system, rather than disrupting all of it. The Affordable Care Act was deeply flawed; had it been a truly great reform, all federal employees, including members of the House and Senate, and of the executive branch would have been the first to enroll. As far as I know, none enrolled. I advocate an open and frank discussion, exploring and exposing all suggestions. If that were to happen, we could possibly arrive at a workable solution leading to a just and fair health care system based on quality of care. I don't believe this will happen anytime soon. My atrabilious opinion is based on the state of the political climate. The two major political parties treat each other with disdain and disrespect. Cooperation has evaporated.

The Social Security system worked perfectly because everyone was required to participate; it would still be working that way if the funds in the lock box had not been raided by the Government. This is one example of why we should be wary of Government control of health care. If in charge, it would be able to change the rules at will, as it did in the case of Social Security.

In a similar fashion, if health care is to function properly, everyone must participate. The lock box must reside in the private sector, and it must come with an iron clad stipulation that it will not, and cannot be raided. The Government must ensure this. These are the general guidelines I would suggest:

- The private sector runs the health care system.
- The Federal government secures the rights of all participants.
- Everyone would be required to participate. Once a person reached the age of 21, he or she would be required to purchase health insurance. There will be exceptions, which I will address later.
- Insurance companies should be encouraged to continue innovating in the variety of plans they can offer to fit the needs of individuals and families. The companies should be able to sell all types of policies across state lines. In addition, other innovative solutions, other than through insurance companies, should be explored.
- Effort would be made to encourage as much competition as possible in order to keep the cost of medical care, insurance, and drugs as low as possible.

How do we handle pre-existing conditions? Since everyone must participate the possibility of not being insured for 50 years, becoming sick, and then demanding to be covered disappears. New born babies would automatically be covered by their parents' policy until age 21. At 21 they would have to buy their own policy and the transition would be seamless. Thus, insurance companies could no longer refuse to cover someone due to a pre-existing condition, because everyone will be covered from birth. The Affordable Care Act mandates that insurance companies must cover those with pre-existing conditions and that provision should be continued in all future plans.

The system must deal fairly and ethically with those who cannot afford insurance, many of whom may never be able to do so. There must also be a provision to support those who become unemployed and cannot afford insurance. Here there must be cooperation between the private sector and the Government to provide assistance and training in order to allow as many as possible to find a job.

The number of U.S. citizens who would be on permanent assistance would be small. Again, cooperation between the private sector and the Government will be necessary to provide funding for a program to support those most in need. Some of the funding could come from a 1% cut in the budgets of every government agency and program. This would have to be done judiciously. The funds would have to be used exclusively for medical coverage for those who cannot afford it themselves.

It is abundantly clear that neither political party has much enthusiasm for developing a great health care system. I believe this is true for three primary reasons: One, if they participate in creating a system in the private sector, it eliminates their great desire for power and control, and closes the door to the abuses of kickbacks and other shenanigans. Two, they would derive no legitimate benefits, which for them is a large disincentive. And three, it would call attention to the fact that they have enjoyed an excellent health care plan all along, and have done very little to help those truly in need. The leadership of the Democrat Party, much more so than the rank and file and the general public, is interested in the

Government totally controlling health care. Only the conservative wing of the Republican Party has offered solutions, but they have been ignored by the party leadership. Sen. Rand Paul has proposed the following:

- A universal health refund that transfers all government tax and spending subsidies to ordinary citizens every year with no strings attached other than the requirement that it be used for health care.
- A flexible health savings account so that money not spent this year can be saved tax free for future medical expenses.
- Protection for people who lose their insurance because of government policies.

These proposals may not solve the problem, but they are worth exploring, along with other suggestions from all parties. The conservative faction is not large enough to control the Republican Party and there is no place else where they can reside. They are too small to support a separate party, and would be rejected by the Democratic Party. While the Democrats have been disingenuous, the Republicans have been injudicious. The two major parties have caused complications and confusion but offered no true solutions.

In closing, I add one final thought. In this country we have the best medical professionals found anywhere around the globe. And with all of its flaws, in my opinion, we still have the best health care system. While some research indicates the U.S. ranks 11th in the world when comparing the best health care systems, the criteria used need to be carefully scrutinized and analyzed. The outcome of such research can change depending on what criteria are used or excluded. If the criteria are relevance, efficiency, effectiveness, impact, sustainability and quality of care, we probably lead in some areas, and lag behind in others. But because our system is largely private, we have the advantage of being much more innovative and creative. Our goal is to improve and perfect our system as much as possible. Highly specialized care, which is not available in many parts of the globe, is available in the United States. Government run health care systems in other countries, at times, require long waiting periods before care is delivered.

Those able to afford it will travel to the U.S. to receive immediate treatment. We should not adopt a mediocre system simply because it is easy; we should work to produce something better. We have many brilliant people with great recommendations; we should explore them all.

CHURCH/RELIGION

"You have made us for yourself and our hearts are restless until they rest in you." Saint Augustine.

Thomas Aquinas, in his volume *On the Truth of the Catholic Faith,* observes that everyone has a desire for perfect happiness which can never be fulfilled in this life but only in the next. Theologians call this the argument for the existence of God from Universal Desire. Peter Kreeft states the argument in more accessible terms:

- "Every natural, innate desire in us corresponds to some real object that can satisfy that desire.

- "But there exists in us a desire which nothing in time, nothing on earth, no creature can satisfy.

- "Therefore, there must exist something more than time, earth and creatures, which can satisfy this desire."

This Universal Desire, existing among all of mankind, has led to the formation of religions. Their adherents have various labels, and are located all over the earth. They may be Jews, Christians, Muslims, Buddhists, Hindi, Taoists, agnostics or even atheists. What unites them is that, knowingly or unknowingly, they are living according to God's laws. Even those who do not belong to a formal organized religion are seeking to fulfill this universal desire. In some cases, those who have no religious affiliation may, in fact, be conducting their lives much more in line with the law of God than those who are members of organized religions but conduct their lives as if the laws of God did not exist. Thus, in a certain sense, all religions can be said to be one because they all seek the same thing.

Given the multiplicity of responses to this universal desire, it is reasonable to conclude that only one of them can be true. As Catholics, we believe it is ours. We believe in the fact that our faith grew out of Judaism. We believe that revelation, scripture and tradition culminated in Jesus the Christ and that all can come to salvation through Jesus. Other religious traditions—Jewish and Muslim for example—would not hold this to be true. Nonetheless, they all believe in God.

Among adherents of all faiths, we generally find somewhat of a tiered system of commitment: Those who are both observant and devout; those who are observant but not devout; below them a tier comprised of members for whom religion has collapsed into a mere social practice. Finally, there are agnostics and atheists who will either have doubts, or deny God altogether. Yet, even their behavior follows the law of God somewhat.

As Catholics we operate from the premise that the law of God is written on our hearts. This opens the possibility that all men can follow the law of God, even if unknowingly. In some cases agnostics or atheists could be pursuing conduct more aligned with the law of God than members of an organized religion who simply pay lip service to their faith. We may ask, "Who is the more faithful friend: The one constantly offering help, but never able to come when the need arises, or the one who never offers help, but comes immediately when the need does arrive?" Labels can either say a lot…or nothing at all.

I am not suggesting that one should not belong to an organized Church. Belonging to a denomination is desirable, but we are all aware of cases where membership is eschewed by individuals for a variety of reasons. One belongs to a specific faith community because one is convinced it has the truth. Thus, each Church/Religion believes itself to be superior to all others. In some cases this opinion is based on arrogance. In most cases the opinion is based on an honest and deeply held belief that one is following the revelation of God and is eager to share the information with their fellow travelers on this earth. Some churches teach that there is only one way to salvation and it is the one they prescribe. God will make the ultimate decision. Our knowledge and understanding is limited; His is not.

As a Catholic, I believe salvation comes through Jesus alone. I do not know if the opportunity to accept Jesus as savior will be afforded to many after death. This is in the hands of God.

We live in a complex and complicated mix of conditions. Evil intent and nefarious practices often win the day, while the just suffer, are ignored and appear to fail. Despair would be the order of the day if not for belief in the Almighty.

Tradition is an important factor in maintaining the strength of the faith, and ensuring its continuing vibrancy in the future. The dangers of ignoring tradition are many and onerous, among them, the loss of the faith by future generations. Blind adherence to tradition also presents its dangers; it can easily set a faulty course which can erode a faith over time, and transform it from an emphasis on God to a mere social practice whose emphasis is on the mundane. Revelation preceded both scripture and tradition. We rely on all three. Practice or tradition follows revelation, and then is solidified in scripture. Scripture then becomes the source of knowledge about the faith. As new practices are proposed or introduced, they should be measured against established revelation, tradition and scripture. If these new practices are found to be violating what has been firmly established in the three categories mentioned above, it should set off alarms in the individual, the community and the Church.

When a culture, a people or a country abandon religion, catastrophic consequences are unleashed. Those seeking to eradicate religion tend to view it as the root of much evil in the world and imagine that, once it has been removed from the human agenda, only what they perceive as benefits will ensue. But the more religion is expunged from humanity, the more devastating problems rear their ugly heads. The destruction of religion brings about the opposite of the intentions of its destructors. The very fact of eliminating religion, which is a sure defense against evil, brings about evil in a multiplicity of forms. This is not a theoretical supposition; we have many examples before our eyes. Nazism and Communism, both atheistic ideologies, have accounted for the deaths of millions. In the more intimate realm, the rise of all of the following can be attributed to the movement away from religious faith: Suicide among the young; abortion; depression; drug abuse; sexual abuse; lack of civility; single parent families; births among unwed mothers; a lack of respect for the past; and a great many other behaviors which are anti-social in nature. Religious belief will not completely eliminate these ills, but it certainly blunts them. Individual behavior will always vary and we will never achieve complete agreement on every issue, no less on individual behavior. But it is certain that, without religious belief, all the ills we seek to eliminate will grow.

The knowledge of God came into the world through the Israelites. God sent His son to the Jewish people and from Judaism sprang Christianity. The Messiah came to save the lost sheep of Israel and, through them, to redeem the rest of mankind. The fulfillment of Judaism is Jesus. He becomes the new Passover, passing over from death to life and in so doing opening the path for us to do the same.

Jesus did not come into the world to form a new religion, and the apostles never thought of themselves as not being faithful Jews. They realized that in Jesus they had come face to face with the Son of God and in Him was the fulfillment of the prophecies in the sacred scripture. Jesus himself tells us that He came to fulfill the law and the prophets. Due to differences in practices, traditions and beliefs we appear to be two separate and different religions. But the source of faith for all of us is the same.

The basis for everything Christians believe derives from God's encounter with His chosen people. This is no less true in what we refer to as the New Testament than it is for the Old Testament; together they comprise Holy Scripture for Christians. Jesus came first to the chosen people and through them to the rest of mankind. The Word of God is operative in many ways in the Old Testament. In the New, the Word takes on the human form of Yeshua or Jesus. Practical divisions will remain, but they are shadows which are obliterated by the brilliance of the underlying truth. Jesus did not come to form a new religion. He himself proclaimed, "Do not think that I have come to abolish the Law or the Prophets; I have not come to abolish them but to fulfill them" (Matthew 5:17). Those who call themselves Christians are proclaiming they believe Jesus to be the Son of God and the Messiah. Yet, they remain deeply rooted in Judaism, i.e. God's calling of all humanity to Himself.

Since I was raised a Catholic, a few words about the Church.

On Earth, the Church is run by men and therefore subject to problems. Its source is God. Its moral teaching is true but, sadly, the practice does not always comport with the Word of God. The Church has had its problems since Vatican II. In my opinion Pope John the XXIII would be highly disappointed with what resulted from his Council. His effort to throw open the windows and let fresh air in ("aggiornamento" in his word) was appropriated by liberal clergy and laity with much damage resulting: The altar rail was removed, eliminating the sense of a holy of holies; the altar was turned around so that the priest now has his back to the real presence of God; the tabernacle is relegated to a side corner rather than being at the center; our ancient tradition of sacred music was abandoned and "elevator music" introduced; the choir was moved out of the choir loft and up to the altar, making them performers rather than ministers, pulling attention away from the altar, rather than enhancing the spiritual aspect. All of these are a capitulation to popular taste, supplying a home-spun picnic atmosphere, keeping everyone in the same place they were in before they walked into the church, rather than taking them to a transcendent place for a brief time. A time which was once used to refresh and invigorate the congregation, preparing them to enter the world with renewed spiritual vigor, is now gone. If you believe I exaggerate, the next time you go to church listen to the cacophony of sound—conversations about all the subjects we should have left outside. This is strange behavior for a group of people who profess with their lips to be in the presence of God but act is if He has left the building. It seems silence, prayer and reflection would be a more appropriate response when in His house. That which once enriched the Mass and attracted a large congregation is gone, replaced with a mundane liturgy and set of rituals which disappoint many.

On the spiritual side, teaching and moral principals have been watered down. In some cases one can hear nonsense being preached from the pulpit by members of the clergy. This does not go unnoticed. One does not need to be highly educated or a biblical scholar in order to be a devout Catholic or person dedicated to God. But even the least educated among us recognizes nonsense or intellectual mush when it is heard. This accommodation of trying to be all things to all people, while watering down the foundations of the faith, is the most dangerous aspect of all the changes in the last forty to fifty years. There is hope that this will change. If significant positive change does not occur, the current trend of followers falling out of the church and into disbelief will continue.

Mercy and Forgiveness

One of the finest gifts we receive from Judaism/ Christianity is the practice of mercy and forgiveness. We see this throughout the entirety of Scripture, which tells us that the Messiah came to redeem us, not to condemn us. Knowing the history of human behavior, past and present, there can be no better example of that behavior than when these two disciplines are in use.

We are likewise called to emulate this behavior. An abundance of mercy and forgiveness among people would do the human race a great deal of good. A caution should be kept in mind. They must be used wisely and judiciously; to practice them fully while abandoning principal and moral law would be a mistake. Misapplying them can cause great harm.

As mentioned earlier, we ought not to judge, but we must evaluate. Practically, that means we can be merciful and forgiving while still holding ourselves accountable for our behavior. There are no free passes or get out of jail free cards. Judgment should remain in the hands of the Almighty who knows the human heart and mind; we are not capable of that. We do not fully understand what God's plan of salvation is. We can petition Him to save all of His creation, but that is out of our hands. Perhaps His plan is to save all of creation; our task, for now, is to practice mercy and forgiveness even for those we oppose, for those who are our enemies, and for those who may have to suffer temporal punishment, such as incarceration for crimes. We easily apply mercy and forgiveness to ourselves, but that does not release us from the fact that we have personal responsibility and duty which must be followed. We are therefore accountable for our actions and justly called to make reparations for our offenses.

If, as Scripture teaches, we love our neighbor as we love ourselves, then how could we not extend the quality of these two practices to our fellows in the same measure we apply them to ourselves. Would we want to be judged by the Lord as we judge each other?

Sin

Here is a word signifying a concept which has been almost completely expunged from the modern vocabulary. Even within the Church there is little reference to sin; the emphasis has shifted almost exclusively to mercy. This shift is ominous and if not adjusted will have seriously negative repercussions. Scripture defines sin very clearly: "Sin is the transgression of the law" (1 John 3:4). It is not just any law which is violated, but the law of God. And while most laws, civil or otherwise, are punitive or restrictive, God's law is prescriptive, and meant to elevate and enhance. It is a law of love. When violated, it is not simply a transgression of a statute, it is a form of treachery and a breach of confidence. This interaction of living in harmony with the law, is not simply one of men with each other, but one which is an interaction of men with the Divine.

I believe that it is fair to say that the wellspring of all sin is pride. Pride allows a dark shadow to pervade both heart and mind; at one and the same time the intellect and the emotions are attacked and overwhelmed. Whether it is fraud, arrogance, violence, myriad abuses or any number of other violations of God's law, at the source is pride. It was the cause of Lucifer's fall, and at a later time, it led to Adam's fall from grace. And, although it is despised by all when seen in others, it holds a particular attraction for each of us.

We are in a constant battle against sin. This is true whether we realize it or not, and it is true even if we have eliminated the concept of sin from our vocabulary or never even considered it. Forces which are beyond our full understanding never rest; they are on a mission of destruction and will continue to pursue their ends until all things are resolved by God. Until then, we must be on guard and realize that we are in a continuing battle which does not cease until we die.

God's hope for us is clear: Jesus tells us we must be perfect as our Heavenly Father is perfect. This objective is viewed by many, even by men of faith, to be unreachable. But it is not an idle command nor is it unreasonable. It is a goal to be working toward. The Lord knows our limitations. He also knows our strengths. All around us, observing human behavior, we see the results of pursuing perfection: Musicians play nearly flawlessly; surgeons operate near the level of perfection; athletes amaze with their abilities. These and many more achievements are examples of what can be accomplished by pursuing perfection. If we were to focus our minds on doing it spiritually, we would help create a better world. No one would be perfect, but if each of us pursued perfection with the full complement of our given endowments, there is no doubt that God would supply the missing portion required to reach perfection. Perhaps it would not happen for everyone during their lifetimes on Earth, but it would eventually happen after death.

The difficult task of avoiding sin remains before us. Different manifestations of sin confront each of us. Satan will always attack the weakest link—the place where we are most vulnerable. We face sin as individuals, but we are not in the battle alone; the immeasurable love of God is with us. If we choose to follow His law, it provides strength enough to be victorious. In addition to mercy, it is vital for the clergy to point out that certain behaviors are sinful. That piece of the puzzle seems to be missing from the current approach.

Time

Leaving physics out of the discussion for now, we experience time in a linear mode. For us, time moves only in one direction, always forward; it is not bi-directional. God is outside of time.

For God there is no past or future, only an eternal present. It may be the point toward which we are moving. We are aware of time because of change, but we do not know exactly what time is, or how to define it. One thing we do know with certainty is that we have a limited supply of it here on earth. Einstein's theory led him to believe there was no difference between past, present and future, no matter how persistent the opposite seemed. It may just be that Einstein's view of time is how it is for God and, eventually, for all the rest of us.

Prayer

Prayer is a communication with the Almighty. The communication moves from God to us, and then back to God. Prayer can be formal, informal or practical, and should not be thought of as being confined to only one of those categories. When we attend a religious ceremony, we experience and participate in formal prayer. Reciting the rosary or other established texts are also examples of formal prayer. When we speak to God in conversation, as we would with a friend, we experience informal prayer. When we live the word of God in the way we conduct our daily lives, we pray a practical prayer. The way we conduct our lives becomes the prayer. If we think of prayer in this way, we realize we must be observant and devout, praying not only in the House of God, but taking it, through example, into the public square. If we think of prayer in this way, every activity in our lives becomes prayer. As a child, when I prayed, I asked God to do things for me. My prayer life has changed significantly since. There are things I ought to do; there are things I need to do; there are things I want to do. Therefore, when I pray, I ask God to give me the wisdom, strength, courage and talent to do them, and all according to His will. We know from the words of Jesus that prayer is extremely powerful. We should not neglect this magnificent gift we have been given. Prayer can be words, thoughts or actions which constantly intermingle as conditions change; each form allows us to live a God centered life. It is difficult for us to believe prayer is as powerful as we are told. And that is not surprising. Even those who were in the presence of Jesus, the Messiah Himself did not fully grasp it; more than once Jesus said to them "Oh, ye of little faith." As we do not have Jesus in our midst, it is even more difficult for us than it was for the disciples. But we should never doubt the awesome power of prayer.

Death

My grandmother was fond of saying that death makes us all equal. It is the one event we know will occur, and we know it a priori. At death we either stand before God, or we go out of conscious existence. Even as a child I knew this life would come to an end and as an adult I am happy to believe in a life after death. If I am wrong, I've lost nothing. If that disconsolate proposition is correct, no matter what I have accumulated or accomplished, all is lost anyway. Believers will ultimately have confirmation of their belief; if the non-believers are correct, none of us will ever know. I believe we will have confirmation rather than not.

How we resolve this issue has profound practical implications. It can mean a life of joy or one of despondence. A serene inner life leads to joy in everything one does. This includes personal advancement and accomplishment, as well as working to build a better world. The effort itself is worthy of praise, even if the result is at times failure. In strictly human terms we have no idea why anything exists at all. Without God, we don't know where we have come from or where we are going, and we don't know what death is. Some live in fear of it all their lives. Without revelation from God we would never have answers to such considerations. God has revealed as much as we need to know at present.

The Bible

When I speak of the Bible I am referring to all of Scripture, what is commonly referred to as the Old and New Testaments. Both should be embraced as one. I am of that opinion because I do not believe God changes; what He revealed to His chosen people still holds true, and Jesus, whom we believe to be the Messiah, confirms as much. A few observations are in order. Most people do not read the bible or use it as a source for guiding the conduct of their lives. There are many reasons for this, among them the fact that the bible can be difficult. Many passages are thorny and difficult to understand. But what is clear throughout is how one should conduct one's life.

There are biblical accounts of violence and murder which many find difficult or impossible to resolve. But the word of God reveals truth: What God has to say about Himself; what He has to say about mankind; what men say about God; and what men say about themselves. All of the perspectives are present, and the misapplication, such as attributing the thinking of men to that of God, or the reverse, will certainly lead to confusion. The attempt to understand can be daunting, and we should consider that we will not understand everything to our satisfaction. This is not an unusual position to be in — there is much we do not understand.

Leaving aside the difficulties for a moment (since they may be well beyond our comprehension) concentrating on the spiritual and moral principles can lead to a richly fulfilling life. For devout Jews and Christians the scripture is the divinely inspired word of God. Because of culture and tradition, each professing group, while respecting the other, disputes the practices and traditions of the other. This is also true of the various branches of Judaism and Christianity. While there is unity in the belief in God, there is much respectful dispute about details. I suspect these will not be resolved before the Messiah comes again.

I am firmly convinced about that coming, and intimate that, at the coming when our eyes and hearts are opened, we will all find we have been wrong in one way or another about some aspect or aspects of our belief. Then we rely on the mercy of God. Now we have His word in scripture and we should do our best to follow it.

● ● ●

Once out of the marina and out to sea, we do not return until the journey's end, an end we have no knowledge of but we know it is a place different than the one from which we started out. For us the adventure began at birth, but never ends.

God

We cannot fully understand God. When Moses asks about God's identity, God replies, "I Am who Am." This is a mystery for us, incomprehensible, since our minds cannot grasp the fact that God is "Being" itself—Ipsum Esse Subsistens. God has always existed, and is in fact the reason there is something rather than nothing. The fact that there is something rather than nothing completely eliminates the concept of absolute nothingness: God is.

Many would agree that there is a "god." What they mean by using the term is a variety of impersonal forces which control the operation of the universe, and those forces are completely indifferent regarding human beings or, for that matter, anything else which exists. The God revealed in the scriptures is a personal God—not a pococurante force, but a loving Father caring for His children. We have a short time on this earth and, when we die, we shall either awake in the presence of God or have gone out of existence. I am convinced we will stand before our creator. The question is, What then?

For us humans, retribution, revenge, reprisal, retaliation—whatever we choose to call it—has been high on the list of our priorities. It is the source of many of our problems and the cause of much sorrow. Scripture indicates that God's priority is salvation. We may have a very limited view of salvation. We have thought about it prominently in reference to humans. But it may be that God's notion of salvation includes much more. And it most certainly has nothing to do with revenge.

We know from scripture that by the time man appears, a fall had already occurred, and spiritual nature was disturbed. We are told Satan and one third of the angels rebelled. The gift of free will was given to mankind and along with it danger and consequences. When misused, man's free will led to the second fall, that of Adam. These two estrangements from God resulted in nature, designed perfectly, being reordered to imperfection. Mankind was now free to do anything it could imagine in heart and mind. This attempt at re-creation in our image may well preclude the return of the Messiah until the possibility of every human behavior has been exhausted. Perhaps by then, realizing there are no further options and that all possibilities have been exhausted, both angels and men will conclude that they now must yield to God's will and acknowledge Him as supreme. In the interim we live with the distortion of nature caused by the fallen angels first, and then, not to be outdone, that of mankind. Crime, war, disease, death and all human problems flow from the one aberration: a voluntary separation from God. Both the fallen angels and mankind chose to misuse the gift of free will, removing themselves from the presence of God. Eventually, even the most cynical among us will tire of all the chaos we have created. It is speculation, but it may just be that God has plans to save all of His creation, including the fallen angels. He sent

Jesus into the physical world to save it, to redeem it and His conception of redemption, salvation and perfection far exceeds anything we can imagine or understand. In spite of the fact that we cannot conceive of evil doers not being punished, perhaps it is a good idea to entertain the possibility that God's plan includes saving all of the fallen angels, all men and, by extension, all He has created. God being perfect, it becomes difficult to envision that He would not ultimately have all of His creation reach perfection. How can this be done? With all the havoc Satan and his cadre have caused, with all the horror men have managed to cause, how can such evil be erased? It may not be possible for any human or angel to comprehend how all the pain, sorrow, grief and horror can be eliminated as if it never occurred. But we are in the presence of Almighty God. I can imagine the day when Jesus returns: Before Him will stand both angels and men, their eyes and hearts open, each repenting, and each accepting the just punishment deserved. And God will be healing every wound as if it never existed, bringing all of His creation back into perfection, as it was in the beginning. This thought, of course, is simply my way of thinking about God's infinite mercy. It is simply a thought or prayer which ends "Thy will be done."

THE ARTS & SCIENCES

Whichever science or art one is immersed in at any particular time...it is the finest among them all. They are all glorious.

Art and science are one; they cannot be separated. We can do so for convenience, but we should always remember art and science are two sides of the same intellectual coin. The brilliance of beauty is supported with technical expertise. And every scientific discovery is the result of creativity and also conveys beauty. This is true of all the arts and sciences. The arts and sciences are as essential to human life as food, clothing and shelter. It is extremely difficult, perhaps impossible to categorize any one of the arts or sciences as the best. Whichever science or art one is immersed in at any particular time, gives the impression that it is the finest among them all. They are all glorious.

Mathematics

The king of the sciences, mathematics plays a part in everything. It is a difficult subject for many, mastered at the highest levels by a few but, in all cases, absolutely essential. It adds to the richness of the human experience. Knowledge of it is essential for progress to occur. Mathematics is, in fact, beautiful. Perhaps not in the same way a painting or piece of music is stunning but, nonetheless, beautiful. Much greater emphasis should be placed on it in the education system, and all students should be encouraged to excel at it. Its presence is felt in music, art and literature, and it is a tool which explains the physical world around us.

Science

Each of the sciences opens for us a world of intellectual beauty and at the same time allows for discoveries which enhance and improve our daily lives. Knowledge, or at least an appreciation, of the sciences is essential. To ignore them is to shortchange one's life. Mathematics, biology, physics, chemistry and many other sciences build the quality of our physical lives. They spur progress and enable the arts to flourish.

Literature

It is one of the most glorious ways in which we use language. It is a vehicle for knowledge, understanding and joy. The lives of countless millions have been enriched and improved by the prose and poetry of the great writers in human history. The importance of reading great literature cannot be over emphasized. The wealth of human emotions, ingenuity and creativity are expressed in our literature; it provides a means of tapping into the wisdom of the ages.

Art

Drawing, painting, sculpture and architecture are among the highest forms of human creativity. They can provide intellectual and emotional satisfaction for the artist and the observer. Encouraging interest in and love of these disciplines should be a high priority in our country. With the advent of instant gratification at our fingertips through the use of iPhones, iPads, and other electronic devices, the impetus to develop the skills necessary to produce great art has been dulled. We should see these devices as tools to be used when necessary, rather than as escape routes or ends in themselves. Art draws us into life and the world around us. If abused, electronic devices tend to create a fantasy world in place of the real one. It is a danger which should be avoided.

Music

Of all the arts music is the most elusive. It can exist in the mind alone or in performance. It is a dynamic art which proceeds in real time. It is the only endeavor from which everyone demands complete perfection from the performers. Those high standards have produced some of the greatest art ever created by the human mind. Mere sound can bring one to smile, cry or dance for joy; there is something magical in that. As with all the arts, the only way to fully appreciate them is to participate in them. In music, that means singing or playing an instrument, not merely listening. One cannot possibly grasp the complexity and subtlety of melody and harmony in the greatest piano literature, for example, without actually playing the pieces oneself. Even if not played at a professional level, working one's way through the music of Bach, Mozart, Beethoven, Schumann, Chopin, Mendelssohn, Brahms, Rachmaninoff, Prokofiev, Bartok, Gershwin and many others will enlighten the mind, refresh the spirit and deepen the appreciation for these amazing geniuses. It will also enhance one's ability to play, since so much of this music will push one beyond one's current capabilities. Pushing the envelope brings rewards.

Many musicians avoid talking about music, and the reason may be what was so well expressed by Leonard Bernstein in his book *The Joy of Music*: "[T]he only way one can really say anything about music is to write music." It expresses so well the fact that sound cannot be properly conveyed by words or any other medium. The classical music genera exemplified by the afore-mentioned composers, along with others too numerous to mention, comprises a body of work which inspires because of its beauty and its ability to communicate with the intellect as well as the emotions. Symphonic music, concertos, opera, chamber music and sacred music have inspired people across the globe. Hopefully, we will be able to keep this music alive and, in the process, produce composers to continue the tradition. Rachmaninoff enunciated it well when he said: "Music is enough for a life time, but a lifetime is not enough for music".

EDUCATION

The ethos of American education has devolved from its beginnings. Its tragic flaw—self-inflicted—is separation from God. The fact that all intelligence, knowledge and wisdom flow from God has been banished. Education happens, but the product is a hollow shell. Technical knowledge is held as superior, but spiritual growth is stunted or non-existent. Thus the system turns out men and women who are sterile utilities rather than caring beings. It was not always the case. A host of other problems which plague the system flow from this "original sin." These problems affect the public system mostly, but they are not confined there: Catholic education, from grammar school through university, has also suffered. Unlike the secular education system, Catholic educators have not knowingly and consciously, with serious purpose, deposed God; but they have unwittingly allowed the secular world to influence the Catholic approach to a spiritual life. Many so called "Catholic" universities are Catholic in name only. And some of what passes for Catholic education in many grammar schools and high schools is so watered down that the Apostles would not recognize it as the gospel proclaimed by Jesus. What passes for religious education in many parish programs is such a juvenile or simplified form of Catholicism that it ends up forfeiting the interest of the students rather than leading them to a deeper understanding of the faith.

Eliminating God from public education has provided fertile soil in which the following intellectual weeds have taken root and flourished:

- Devaluing instruction in history, our connection to our roots;
- The conviction that man by himself can bring about a utopia, given sufficient time;
- The idea that truth is variable — subjective not objective;
- Any and all means can be used to achieve a goal;
- One should always avoid any reference to death;
- One should always avoid any reference to sin;
- Never let facts dominate your feelings;
- Make everyone feel comfortable just as they are;
- Promote any fad or agenda, true or not, which consolidates the power of the elitists;
- Do not question authority;
- Civil authorities will determine, selectively, which behaviors are equal, just different in kind.

This list of destructive propositions, which is by no means exhaustive, has given us schools which fail to educate academically as well as morally. Poor education goes on to afflict the wider society while one of the key sources of the problem, the schools' performance, is rarely addressed. In that wider society, the results are clearly seen and felt. Deficiency, in academics and morality, leads to increased violent crime rates, drug and alcohol abuse, domestic violence, suicide and a host of other ills. An unhealthy concentration on sports, and the relentless pursuit of material goods are readily observable. In lieu of playing video games and devoting hours of their lives to passively watching cell phones, iPads and computers, both children and adults could be actively learning to play a musical instrument, writing poetry, painting, sculpting or otherwise developing their God given talents thus enriching the world around them. This will not happen by following the propositions listed above.

As I implied earlier, our education system was not always divorced from God. In fact, most universities in the United States were established as faith based institutions: Harvard, Yale, Dartmouth, William & Mary, Princeton, Rutgers and many others had their roots in religion.

Alexis de Tocqueville traveled to the United States in 1831; he codified his observations in *Democracy in America* in 1835. Here are two quotes of his about the importance of religion in our country:

"In America religion is the road to knowledge, and the observance of the divine laws leads man to civil freedom."

"Liberty cannot be established without morality, nor morality without faith."

What happened? Why did this separation occur? There are many reasons, but my interest is less focused on them, than on restoring God to His rightful place in our education system. What is seen as progress, is merely elevating mediocrity to a position it does not deserve. Unfortunately this has happened throughout the society at large and, more tragically, in the churches themselves — including the Catholic Church.

Where are we headed? Where do we go from here? Can this situation be corrected? These are some of the questions which come to mind. It is impossible to predict what correction will be made or if one will even be attempted. My own thoughts are these: Public education will not change any time soon, if ever. Religious education will be subject to a pendulum motion, moving between liberal and conservative approaches depending on who wields the power and influence. As throughout history, this state of affairs will continue until God sends His Holy Spirit to enlighten educators and get the system back on the correct path.

For all of society, religious or secular, there is a universally crucial consideration. Working from the general society to the particular of education we can say the following: If there is a God, then we are required to act a certain way. If there is no God, we then may act as we please. Applied to education, if there is a God, then we must educate in a certain way; if there is no God, we can educate any way we like. I would submit the God way leads to success; the other is doomed to failure. As it stands now, both secular and religious education needs reform. All education in the public sector has long since reached the stage that, estranged from God, the system allows for any and every possible mistake. Some of the problems created have been and will continue to be innocuous; some have been and will continue to be disastrous. In many cases this is equally true of Catholic education. Ineffective and erroneous moral and religious instruction has also damaged regular academic subject matter. That is to say the subject matter itself is accurate, but it has been cut off from its source. And that allows for misapplication, or misuse of the subject matter. It removes the moral component from consideration of how it is to be used.

Mixed messages from the clergy about the Gospel of Jesus have led to fuzzy doctrinal teaching, in turn leading to confusion among students. A telling result is, students come away from religious education without a clear understanding of their faith and down play its importance. A recent survey found that 70% of Catholics do not believe that bread and wine are changed into the Body and Blood of Jesus at the Consecration. Of these, 35% say they had never been taught that. Either they were not paying attention or the teaching has gone very wrong. If in fact the adoption of the ecumenically naïve notion of "go along, get along" is firmly fixed in the Church's religious education programs, then we are indeed in a great deal of trouble.

At present, no reform is possible in the public educational system. We can only attempt to influence it through the example provided by the Catholic model. However, there is a problem: Before the Catholic model can provide a positive influence on the rest of society, it must first clean its own house. In broad terms, the Catholic model seems to have lost confidence in its own efficacy. And this may be a result of abandoning its traditions which are thousands of years old. As a first step, Catholic education needs to adopt the attitude of influencing all education rather than allowing non-religious models to influence it. Minus this, the descent of education will continue. Once the correction is made in Catholic education, a concerted effort must be undertaken to influence the vast world of education. A large part of this will include a rededication to proclaiming the Gospel of Jesus to the whole world. Much of that should be done by the example of the way in which we conduct our lives. This may not provide a guarantee, but it will provide a hope of success. The correction needed will come with the guidance of the Holy Spirit at a time God wills.

Education cannot be separated from God simply because some organization or system declares it so. God is the source of all education. "Without God," means without foundation. It also means replacing God with man. Such a design has little hope of success. Furthermore, even in those influenced by the most manipulated or distorted forms of education, there will be a nagging yearning for something which is felt to be missing. Truth, even if repressed, is always lurking in the background. Adjustments to curriculum and methods, a return to discipline, higher standards and even a return to prayer will be window dressing without a sense of the Divine. Throughout human history, every civilization has had some sense of the transcendent. In the 20th century, after World War I, and World War II and into the 21st Century, this sense has been steadily eroded. It remains to be seen whether or not we can regain that ancient wisdom.

The attempt to reform all education must be made, even though it appears to be an impossible task. It must come from the Catholic School system, and that effort must be forcibly and actively supported by clergy and laity alike. There is a method which has worked in every age and in every culture throughout history. Though it has been practiced only among limited groups, it has produced much success. Honest and dedicated teachers, principals and parents, working together to educate each student to his or her full potential while acknowledging God's role in the process, should be brought into the entire education establishment by the Catholic school system.

A BRIEF WORD

Ostensibly, it initially appeared we were in for a sailing adventure at sea. One could ask how we went so far off course, but in fact we did not. You are the lone sailboat; I am the lone sailboat; every one of us through all ages and places on earth and continuing into the future are lone sailboats. The timeless issues explored in this essay are faced by each of us privately and silently, as it has been since we have been on the earth and will continue into the future for a time not determined by us. We all live in a community. We are supported, helped and interact with family, friends and the community at large. But we make choices about the crucial issues discussed herein as individuals. We may seek the wisdom and advice of others, but ultimately we make the decision alone. We did not will ourselves to be alive or to be lone sailboats, but we do will the way in which we navigate that vessel.

These considerations are universal. We may have been nurtured in a God centered life from childhood, come to faith along the way, lost faith along the way or never had or wanted faith. What we share in common is the fact that these issues proffer themselves to us unsolicited. The quality of life we have, both internally and externally, is determined by how we address the issues. All of the issues I have addressed reflect my encounter with reality during my brief time on earth. They are not idle opinions; they have a foundation in the reality I perceive around me, and from the revelation we have from Sacred Scripture. I firmly hold the convictions I have expressed but, having said that, I am always open to correction. And I am always willing to listen and consider an argument contrary to mine. I would like to be in the category which William Buckley comically quipped about himself saying: "Everybody makes mistakes, and one day I believe I may even make one." I am far from being without mistakes. I hope in all that I have said I have not made the mistake of offering offense to anyone in any way; that is furthest from my intent.

One final note: If you find this book at all to your liking, it will be due, in so small part, to the excellent editing, design recommendations, and many other superb observations, suggestions and advice provided by my editor, Christopher Brune.

Edward Dorozynski

CPSIA information can be obtained
at www.ICGtesting.com
Printed in the USA
BVHW042255070721
611306BV00006B/187